The Days
and the Nights

Prayers for Women

The Days and the Nights

Prayers for Women

Collected
by
Candida Lund

THOMAS MORE PRESS
Chicago, Illinois

ISBN: 0-88347-089-6

———————

The author wishes to thank the following for
permission to include lines from the following
publications:

Abbey Press: "A Wife's Prayer" by Abbey Press.
Copyright © 1965 by Abbey Press.

Central Conference of American Rabbis: From
GATES OF PRAYER, edited by Rabbi Chaim Stern.
Copyright © 1975 by the Central Conference of
American Rabbis.

Collins Publishers: "Prayer of a Woman Living
Alone" and "Expecting a Baby" from A WOMAN'S
BOOK OF PRAYERS by Rita Snowden. Copyright ©
1958 by Rita F. Snowden.

The Crossing Press: "For the Woman Who Asked
Me If I Believe In God and If I Pray" from
MOUNTAIN MOVING DAY, edited by Elaine Gill.
Copyright © 1973 by The Crossing Press.

The John Day Company: From ONCE UPON A
CHRISTMAS by Pearl S. Buck. Copyright © 1950,
1956, 1957, 1960 by Pearl S. Buck. Copyright ©
1969 by the Pearl S. Buck Foundation, Inc.
Copyright © 1956, 1962, 1967, 1971, 1972 by
Creativity, Inc.

And God called the light Day,
and the darkness he called Night.

— Genesis

. . . every day is all there is.

— Joan Didion (in an interview)

Preface

Because this is a prayerbook for women it does not necessarily follow that its prayers have been written by women and for women. Rather, it means that it is a selection of prayers collected by one woman, contentedly and gratefully conscious of being a woman, who thinks that this collection may help to voice the concerns, joys, hopes, and fears that mark the days and nights of many of us. Not all the prayers are for everyone, nor is any one prayer suitable for all times.

Why a prayerbook specifically for women? In her splendid book, *What a Modern Catholic Believes About Women,* Sister Albertus Magnus McGrath writes:

Women must prove themselves in confidence and in freedom in their lives in the church and in all other aspects of their lives. What they have the ability to do is what they should do, and should fight for the opportunity to do. If women are to be taken seriously when they demand full recognition in the Church, they must live truly responsible and strong religious, personal, and professional lives. They must work out in their own business and social lives, in culture, politics, and marriage what the meaning of the Gospel message is in their complex human situation, without much expectation of, or dependence on, help from authoritative voices which will comfort them that they are "right". This requires that they deepen their own

theological knowledge, come in living contact with the
Scriptures, be firm in personal decision, *untiring in
prayer.* [Emphasis mine]

The thrust of Sister Albertus Magnus'
observation is that it is all up to us as women.

It is we who are able to judge more
accurately what prayers best fit our lives. We
who need to choose language meaningful to us
and not permit ourselves to be penned in by
the mawkish and maudlin. We who best know
what strengthens us. We who best realize our
own potentialities. We who best recognize
what we have already actualized. These are
some reasons why there should be a
prayerbook for women.

Certainly such a prayerbook does not have
as part of its rationale that we women are
more prayerful than men. This argument
would be selfish and chauvinistic; in short,
unfair. Often, however, women are more
aware than men of social change. We do not
allow ourselves cocoons of comfort. We
recognize tensions, stress, crises, change, in
our lives and in the lives of those dear to us.
We cry out for ourselves and for them, and we
want to translate our cries into prayers. We
cannot, however, always find the kind of
prayers we wish.

It has become harder and harder to pray.
Conversely, prayer has become increasingly
necessary for our happiness. It may be that we
need to learn a new way to pray. Some have

stopped praying altogether, turning instead to psychological gimmicks. Traditional prayers, too often, have been artificial and fawning, and have left twentieth century women feeling uncomfortable. Too often, on the other hand, we moderns have attempted to dissect prayer: how does it work; does it make any difference; what does it accomplish? Dissection is not the answer.

This collection provides a new/old way to pray. It also reflects a conviction of mine that prayer should be a very natural, supernatural exercise—one of the most natural things we do. St. Thomas Aquinas put it another way. He said that grace builds on nature, a very comforting thought. We should pray as we naturally are. If sham and pretense are to be shunned in exchanges with one another how can we think of being anything but ourselves with God. We should let our prayers mirror ourselves whether those selves be slow and plodding, clever and witty, steady and confident, frightened and uncertain, joyous and lyrical. We need to be ourselves when we pray so that our prayers will be a natural outpouring of selves to God who made us as we are. Prayer should be as natural to us as conversation (although admittedly the inarticulate too can find comfort in prayer), and thus it becomes more than dutiful chores or the futile striving for something we do not understand.

If well-meaning hagiographers have not been guilty of spiritual malpractice at least they may have been guilty of misleading many of us by implying that prayer can only be an esoteric exercise, transporting one to realms almost beyond comprehension—and to which not everyone should feel called. They have indeed propagated a type of holy snobbism. I have no quarrel with the kind of heights reached by certain mystics. I only emphasize that we are not all mystics, and since Christ told us that we ought always to pray this indicates that we must not be ashamed of being ourselves and using words that come naturally to us whether they are our own or another's.

Purposely, I have chosen the prayers for this book from a wide variety of sources. I like seeing that through the centuries people in different roles and different conditions have in distinct ways lifted their hearts to God. To know this strengthens my own prayer. Furthermore, I have not always chosen traditionally structured prayers, but have also included poems, letters, diary-excerpts, and expressions of transcendent thought, for to me these too are legitimate forms of prayers, sometimes even more legitimate.

Candida Lund
Rosary College
May, 1977

We have to begin to see what Christianity really is, that "our God is a living fire; though He slay me yet will I trust Him." We have to think in terms of the Beatitudes and the Sermon on the Mount and have this readiness to suffer. "We have not yet resisted unto blood." We have not yet loved our neighbor with the kind of love that is a precept to the extent of laying down our life for him. And our life very often means our money, money that we have sweated for; it means our bread, our daily living, our rent, our clothes. We haven't shown ourselves ready to lay down our life. This is a new precept, it is a new way. . . . I always comfort myself by saying that Christianity is only two days old (a thousand years are as one day in the sight of God) and so it is only a couple of days that are past and now it is about time we began to take these things literally, to begin tomorrow morning and say, "Now I have begun."

Dorothy Day
(1899-   )
We Must Begin

What will befall us to-day, O God, we know not; we only know that nothing will happen which Thou has not foreseen, determined, desired, and ordered—that is enough for us. Thee do we worship and adore. We ask in the name of Jesus Christ our Saviour, and through His infinite merits, patience in all our sufferings, perfect submission to Thee for all that Thou desirest or permittest, guidance in all that we undertake; for Thine honour and glory we ask it.   Amen.

Princess Elizabeth of France
(1764-1794)

All night I suffered, all night my body trembled to deliver its offering. There is the sweat of death on my temples; but it is not death, it is life!

And I call you now Infinite Sweetness, God, that you release it gently.

Let it be born! And let my cry of pain rise in the dawn, braided into the singing of birds!

Gabriela Mistral
(1889-1957)
Dawn

This is my prayer, O God, today—
That Thou wilt teach me how to pray.

For I would learn in everything
I do or think or hope or sing—

To praise Thee, and this is my prayer
To love Thee always, everywhere.

Mary Dixon Thayer
(1896-   )

Mother of God, there still is pain,
Still is regret, there still is longing,
The sad, soft bitterness of rain,
The faces of those we have been wronging.

Mother of God, you and your child
Have only simple and deep emotions,
But there are nights when winds run wild,
And tumult disconcerts the oceans.

Augustine Bowe
(1892-1966)
But There Are Nights

O God, make the door of this house wide enough to receive all who need human love and fellowship; narrow enough to shut out all envy, pride and strife.

Make its threshold smooth enough to be no stumbling-block to children, nor to straying feet, but rugged and strong enough to turn back the tempter's power. God make the door of this house the gateway to thine eternal kingdom.

St. Stephen's, Walbrook, London

O God, I live alone like many in this city, this country.
I do my own work, I go in and out, I think my own thoughts.
I am friendly to those I know, but nobody knows me as you do.
And nobody anywhere is so close and so understanding.
Bless all those I know who live alone from choice,
All who live alone following a death,
All who live alone because of estrangement,
All who live alone for financial reasons.
Bless each small room I think of, each flat, each too large old house,

Wherever one raises her voice to you in
     prayer at any time.
Bless especially, any one of us who has
     grown shy, selfish, or odd.
Anyone who would like to change, but feels
     she can't; anyone ill, or frail.
Some of us are young still and we enjoy
     freedom,
   We go out and we come in—we visit and
     have visitors;
   We are happy to surround ourselves with
     beauty;
   We enjoy our meals and flowers and pretty
     things.
Single, married, divorced—young, middle-
     aged, old—we are all your children, part
     of your great human family. All the time,
     we need courage and reassurance and
     your loving care and presence. Keep us.
Amen.

Rita Snowden
(1907-   )
Prayer of a Woman Living Alone

Watch, O Lord, with those who wake,
  or watch, or weep tonight, and give your
  angels and saints charge over those
  who sleep.
Tend our sick ones, O Lord Christ.
Rest your weary ones,
Bless your dying ones,
Soothe your suffering ones,
Pity your afflicted ones,
Shield your joyous ones,
And all for your love's sake.   Amen.

St. Augustine
(354-430)

I'm not good," Helena said. "I've never been
very good. My husband used to say he never
felt at home with too good people. 'Let's not
be too good, Helena,' he used to say. 'Let's
just be decent and kind, so God can use us.
I'm sure He can't use people who are too
much like Him.' I always loved my husband
when he said that."

Mary Ellen Chase
(1887-1973)
A Journey to Boston

Christopher, come back to earth again.
There is no age in history when men
So cried for you, Saint of a midnight wild,
Who stood beside a stream and heard a child.
Not even Francis, brother to the poor,
Who, barefoot, begged for alms from door
    to door,
And pity-tortured kissed the leper's brow—
Not even Francis is so needed now
As you, Christ-bearer.

Anne Morrow Lindbergh
(1906-   )
Saint For Our Time

And in the evening, when I lie in bed and
end my prayers with the words, "I thank you,
God, for all that is good and dear and
beautiful," I am filled with joy. Then I think
about "the good" of going into hiding, of my
health and with my whole being of the "dear-
ness" of Peter, of that which is still embryonic
and impressionable and which we neither of us
dare to name or touch, of that which will come
sometime; love, the future, happiness and of
"the beauty" which exists in the world; the
world, nature, beauty and all, all that is
exquisite and fine.

I don't think then of all the misery, but of

the beauty that still remains. This is one of the things that Mummy and I are so entirely different about. Her counsel when one feels melancholy is: "Think of all the misery in the world and be thankful that you are not sharing in it!" My advice is: "Go outside, to the fields, enjoy nature and the sunshine, go out and try to recapture happiness in yourself and in God. Think of all the beauty that's still left in and around you and be happy!"

I don't see how Mummy's idea can be right, because then how are you supposed to behave if you go through the misery yourself? Then you are lost. On the contrary, I've found that there is always some beauty left—in nature, sunshine, freedom, in yourself; these can all help you. Look at these things, then you find yourself again, and God, and then you regain your balance.

And whoever is happy will make others happy too. He who has courage and faith will never perish in misery!

Anne Frank
(1929-c.1945)

My soul doth magnify the Lord.
And my spirit hath rejoiced in God
    my Saviour.
For he hath regarded the low estate of his
    handmaiden:
for, behold, from henceforth all generations
    shall call me blessed.
For he that is mighty hath done to me great
    things; and holy is his name.
And his mercy is on them that fear him
    from generation to generation.
He hath shewed strength with his arm; he
    hath scattered the proud in the
    imagination of their hearts.
He hath put down the mighty from their seats,
    and exalted them of low degree.
He hath filled the hungry with good things;
    and the rich he hath sent empty away.
He hath helped his servant Israel, in
    remembrance of his mercy;
As he spake to our fathers, to Abraham,
    and to his seed for ever.

      St. Luke
      (1st Century)
      The Magnificat

Jesus, Saviour of human activity to which You have given meaning, Saviour of human suffering to which You have given living value, be also the Saviour of human unity; compel us to discard our pettinesses, and to venture forth, resting upon You, into the uncharted ocean of charity.

Pierre Teilhard de Chardin
(1881-1955)

There is but one road which reaches God and that is prayer; if anyone shows you another, you are being deceived.

St. Teresa of Avila
(1515-1582)

Grant us grace, Almighty Father, so to pray as to deserve to be heard.

Jane Austen
(1775-1817)

Help me Lord, not only to appreciate my friends but, like you, to be a friend: to give as well as receive, to be alert and available to them as you were. Bless each of those whom you have placed in my life's pathway, and who brighten the dark days with their friendship, and make the bright days even more beautiful through their generosity, and graciousness. Each is a reflection of you, Lord, and through them I have learned to know you better, for we love God with the same hearts with which we love our friends. Thank you for giving them to me, so that I have learned to love.

Sister Hester Valentine
(1909-   )

Forgive him, Lord, his letter to Timothy:
"Let a woman learn in silence with
        submissiveness.
For I do not allow a women to teach,
or to hold any authority over men.
She is to keep quiet.
For Adam was created first then Eve.
And it was not Adam who was fooled by
        the serpent,
but it was the woman who led him into sin.
Yet, women can be saved by child-bearing

if they continue in faith and love and
    holy modesty."
The exegetes can try to explain that one
    away all they like.
The truth is that here Paul was just a pioneer
in the Church's long trek away from the
    words and example of Jesus
who proclaimed no division of his love
    by gender,
who loved Mary as he did John.
It was not a woman who betrayed him,
nor a female who denied him or ran away
    from the cross.
That petulant little note should have been
    returned to sender.
I only trust that Paul's reward in heaven is
    interrupted now and then,
By the non-submissive conversations of
    some ladies
Who, in spite of him, got in.

Sean Freeman
(1930-   )
For Paul, the Chauvinist

Dear Father, help me with the love
    That casteth out all fear;
Teach me to lean on Thee, and feel
    That Thou are very near;
That no temptation is unseen,
    No childish grief too small,
Since Thou, with patience infinite,
    Dost soothe and comfort all.

Louisa May Alcott
(1833-1888)

O Love, come to my help; be my ambassador with God; deign to get for me the grace of devotion.

Take into Thy keeping every good thing which I have been able to do; that they may become the better for Thy custody.

Be near to me, O Love, and help me in all my toil and tribulation; so that I may not feel the heaviness of labour, nor sink under adversity.

St. Gertrude
(1256-1302)

Life is too short," I have often been warned.
I am aware of the importance of every second.
Short, yet time for accomplishments.
Realizing death is near, I find no reason to fear.
I have seen beautiful glimmers of heaven.
I look forward to Your kingdom.

Please, God, let me find myself first.
What individual am I?
What is the meaning of Love?
Let death wait until then.

Laurie Spitzig
(1960-   )

Christ be with me, Christ within me,
Christ before me, Christ beside me.
    Christ to win me,
Christ to comfort and restore me,
Christ beneath me, Christ above me,
Christ in quiet, Christ in danger,
Christ in hearts of all that love me,
Christ in mouth of friend and stranger.

St. Patrick
(c.385-461)

Let nothing disturb you,
Nothing affright you;
All things are passing,
God never changes.
Patience endurance
Attains to all things;
Who God possesses
In nothing is wanting;
Alone God suffices.

> St. Teresa of Avila
> (1515-1582)

Live your life while you have it. Life is a splendid gift. There is nothing small in it. For the greatest things grow by God's law out of the smallest. You must not fritter it away in "fair purpose, erring act, inconstant will"; but must make your thoughts, your words, your acts, all work to the same end, and that end not self, but God. That is what we call *character.*

> Florence Nightingale
> (1820-1910)

Why should I worry?
It's not by busines to think of myself.
My business is to think of God.
It's His business to think of me.

Simone Weil
(1909-1943)

O gracious and holy Father, give us
Wisdom to perceive thee;
Intelligence to understand thee;
Diligence to seek thee;
Patience to wait for thee;
Eyes to behold thee;
A heart to meditate upon thee;
And a life to proclaim thee:
    through the power of the Spirit of Jesus
        Christ our Lord.   Amen.

St. Benedict
(c.480-c.547)

Keep us, O God, from all pettiness; let us be large in thought, in word, in deed.

Let us be done with fault finding and leave off all self seeking.

May we put away all pretense and meet each other face to face without self-pity and without prejudice.

May we never be hasty in judgment and always generous.

Let us take time for all things, and make us to grow calm, serene, and gentle.

Teach us to put into action our better impulses, straight forward and unafraid.

Grant that we may realize that it is the little things of life that create differences, that in the big things of life, we are as one.

And, O Lord God, let us not forget to be kind! Amen.

Mary Stuart, Queen of Scotland
(1542-1587)

Prayer is the place of refuge for every worry,
a foundation for cheerfulness,
a source of constant happiness,
a protection against sadness
and depression of the soul.

St. John Chrysostom
(c.347-407)

Lord, make me an instrument of your peace;
where there is hatred, let me sow love;
where there is injury, pardon;
where there is doubt, faith;
where there is despair, hope;
where there is darkness, light;
and where there is sadness, joy.

Grant that I may not so much seek to be
consoled as to console;
to be understood, as to understand,
to be loved as to love;
for it is in giving that we receive,
it is in pardoning that we are pardoned,
and it is in dying that we are born
to eternal life.

St. Francis of Assisi
(c.1182-1226)

Because I believe that God is new every morning, I believe that God is creating the world today, at this very moment. He did not just create it in the long ago and then forget about it. That means that we have to expect the unexpected as the normal way God's Providence is at work.

That "unexpected" of God is exactly what saves and liberates us from determinism and from the sociologism of gloomy statistics about the state of human affairs in the present. That "unexpected," since it comes from God, is something coming out of his love for us, for the betterment of his children.

I am hopeful, not for human reasons or because I am optimistic by nature, but because I believe in the Holy Spirit present in his Church and in the world—even if people don't know his name. I am hopeful because I believe that the Holy Spirit is still the creating Spirit, and that he will give us every morning fresh freedom, joy and a new provision of hope, if we open our soul to him.

. . . .

Hope is a duty, not just a nicety. Hope is

not a dream, but a way of making dreams become reality.

Happy those who dream dreams and are ready to pay the price to make them become true!

L. J. Cardinal Suenens
(1904-   )

When the signs of age begin to mark my body (and still more when they touch my mind); when the ill that is to diminish me or carry me off strikes from without or is born within me; when the painful moment comes in which I suddenly awaken to the fact that I am ill or growing old; and above all at that last moment when I feel I am losing hold of myself and am absolutely passive within the hands of the great unknown forces that have formed me; in all those dark moments, O God, grant that I may understand that it is You (provided only my faith is strong enough) who are painfully parting the fibres of my being in order to penetrate to the very marrow of my substance and bear me away within yourself.

The more deeply and incurable the evil is encrusted in my flesh, the more it will be You that I am harbouring—You as a loving, active principle of purification and detachment. The more the future opens before me like some dizzy abyss or dark tunnel, the more confident I may be—if I venture forward on the strength of Your word—of losing myself and surrendering myself in You, of being assimilated by Your body, Jesus.

. . . Vouchsafe, therefore, something more precious still than the grace for which all the faithful pray. It is not enough that I should die while communicating. Teach me to treat my death as an act of communion.

> Pierre Teilhard de Chardin
> (1881-1955)
> *Communion Through Diminishment*

Lord, lift us out of Private-mindedness and give us Public souls to work for Thy Kingdom by daily creating that Atmosphere of a happy temper and generous heart which alone can bring the Great Peace.

> Bishop Hacket
> (17th Century)

I

They say that God lives very high;
  But if you look above the pines
You cannot see our God;—and why?

II

And if you dig down in the mines
  You never see Him in the gold;
Though from Him all that's glory shines.

III

God is so good, He wears a fold
  Of heaven and earth across His face—
Like secrets kept, for love, untold.

IV

But still I feel that His embrace
  Slides down by thrills, through all things
    made,
Through sight and sound of every place:

V

As if my tender mother laid
  On my shut lips her kisses' pressure,

Half-waking me at night, and said
  "Who kissed you through the dark, dear
  guesser?"

Elizabeth Barrett Browning
(1806-1861)
A Child's Thought of God

O Christmas, come, when our tall sons need
not face the darkening future and life cut off!
O Christ Child, show us that such things need
not be! We are so skilled in war, so fumbling
in the ways of making peace. We choose the
easy way, and for this we shall not be forgiven.
Of those to whom much is given, much is
expected. At Christmastime I know again
what I have always known. In the midst of joy,
in the safety of our home, among our living
children, I feel the anger of the world descend
upon us, who have been given much, and yet
have not found the ways of peace. The old wise
words come back to me again, "The inferior
man blames others, but the superior man ever
blames himself."

Pearl Buck
(1892-1974)
Once Upon A Christmas

Most glorious Lord of life, that on this day
  Didst make thy triumph over death and sin;
  And having harrowed hell didst bring away
  Captivity thence captive, us to win:
This joyous day, dear Lord, with joy begin,
  And grant that we for whom thou didst
    die
  Being with thy dear blood clean washed
    from sin,
  May live forever in felicity.

Edmund Spenser
(1552-1599)
Easter

Glory be to God for dappled things—
  For skies of couple-colour as a brinded cow;
    For rose-moles all in stipple upon trout
    that swim;
Fresh firecoal chestnut-falls; finches' wings;
  Landscapes plotted and pieced-fold, fallow,
    and plough;
    And all trades, their gear and tackle and
    trim.

All things counter, original, spare, strange;

Whatever is fickle, freckled (who knows
      how?)
      With swift, slow; sweet, sour; adazzle,
      dim;
He fathers-forth whose beauty is past change:
            Praise him.

                  Gerard Manley Hopkins
                  (1844-1889)
                  Pied Beauty

Help me to see! not with my mimic sight—
      With yours! which carried radiance, like
            the sun,
Giving the rays you saw with—light in light—
      Tying all suns and stars and worlds in one.

Help me to know! not with my mocking art—
      With you, who knew yourself unbound by
            laws;
Gave God your strength, your life, your sight,
      your heart,
      And took from him the Thought that Is—
            the Cause.

Help me to feel! not with my insect sense,—
      With yours that felt all life alive in you;

Infinite heart beating at your expense;
   Infinite passion breathing the breath
      you drew!

Help me to bear! not my own baby load,
   But yours; who bore the failure of the light,
The strength, the knowledge and the thought
      of God,—
   The futile folly of the Infinite!

         Henry Adams
         (1838-1918)
         Prayer to the Virgin of Chartres

O sing unto the Lord a new song: sing unto
the Lord, all the earth.

Sing unto the Lord, bless his name; shew
forth his salvation from day to day.

Declare his glory among the heathen, his
wonders among all people.

For the Lord *is* great, and greatly to be
praised; he *is* to be feared above all gods.

For all the gods of the nations *are* idols: but
the Lord made the heavens.

Honour and majesty *are* before him:
strength and beauty *are* in his sanctuary.

Give unto the Lord, O ye kindreds of the people, give unto the Lord glory and strength.

Give unto the Lord the glory *due unto* his name: bring an offering, and come into his courts.

O worship the Lord in the beauty of holiness: fear before him, all the earth.

Say among the heathen *that* the Lord reigneth: the world also shall be established that it shall not be moved: he shall judge the people righteously.

Let the heavens rejoice, and let the earth be glad; let the sea roar, and the fulness thereof.

Let the field be joyful, and all that *is* therein: then shall all the trees of the wood rejoice.

Before the Lord: for he cometh, for he cometh to judge the earth: he shall judge the world with righteousness, and the people with his truth.

David
(c.1060-c.972 B.C.)
Psalm 96

Blessed Trinity have pity!
  You can give the blind man sight,
Fill the rocks with waving grasses—
  Give my house a child tonight.

You can bend the woods with blossom,
  What is there you cannot do?
All the branches burst with leafage,
  What's a little child to you?

Trout out of a spawning bubble,
  Bird from shell and yolk of an egg,
Hazel from a hazel berry—
  Jesus, for a son I beg!

Corn from shoot and oak from acorn
  Miracles of life awake,
Harvest from a fist of seedlings—
  Is a child so hard to make?

Childless men although they prosper
  Are praised only when they are up,
Sterile grace however lovely
  Is a seed that yields no crop.

There is no hell, no lasting torment
   But to be childless at the end,
A naked stone in grassy places,
   A man who leaves no love behind.

God I ask for two things only,
   Heaven when my life is done,
Payment as befits a poet—
   For my poem pay a son.

Plead with Him O Mother Mary,
   Let Him grant the child I crave,
Womb that spun God's human tissue,
   I no human issue leave.

Brigid after whom they named me,
   Beg a son for my reward,
Let no poet empty-handed
   Leave the dwelling of his lord.

        Giollabhrighde MacConmidhe
        (Late 13th Century)
        Childless

Down by the rushes I paused and bent—
I bent with a sudden lovely pang of joy,
And I knew that my hope was true. . . .
Lord God of our fathers, if thou send me a son
He shall be bred in thy fear,
But if thou send me a daughter
She shall be bred in thy love.
Lord, I pray thee, send me a girl.

> Sheila Kaye-Smith
> (1887-1956)
> *The Conception B. V.M.*

Oh, help me, God! For Thou alone
Cans't my distracted soul relieve;
Forsake it not: it is Thine own,
Though weak, yet longing to believe.

Oh, drive those cruel doubts away;
And make me know that Thou art God!
A faith, that shines by night and day,
Will lighten every earthly load.

> Anne Brontë
> (1820-1849)
> *The Doubter's Prayer*

This, could I paint my inward sight,
This were Our Lady of the Night:

She bears on her front's lucency
The starlight of her purity:

For as the white rays of that star
The union of all colours are,

She sums all virtues that may be
In her sweet light of purity.

The mantle which she holds on high
Is the great mantle of the sky.

Think, O sick toiler, when the night
Comes on thee, sad and infinite,

Think, sometimes, 'tis our own Lady
Spreads her blue mantle over thee,

And folds the earth, a wearied thing,
Beneath its gentle shadowing;

Then rest a little; and in sleep
Forget to weep, forget to weep!

Francis Thompson
(1859-1907)
*Lines for a Drawing of
Our Lady of the Night*
45

Lord Jesus Christ,
you are for me medicine when I am sick;
you are my strength when I need help;
you are life itself when I fear death;
you are the way when I long for heaven;
you are light when all is dark;
you are my food when I need nourishment!

St. Ambrose
(c.340-397)

You know who said "I am the Way, the
Truth and the Life," and "he who follows Me
walks not in darkness but in light." And the
Church is His bride, the faithful . . . of the
Church are they who prefer to suffer death a
thousand times than to leave it. If you reply
that it looks as though the Church must
surrender, for it is impossible for it to save
itself and its children, I say to you that it is not
so. The outward appearance deceives, but look
at the inward, and you will find that it
possesses a power which its enemies can never
possess.

St. Catherine of Siena
(1347-1380)

46

The secret of my identity is hidden in the love and mercy of God.

But whatever is in God is really identical with Him: for His infinite simplicity admits no division and no distinction. Therefore I cannot hope to find myself anywhere except in Him.

Ultimately the only way that I can be myself is to become identified with Him in Whom is hidden the reason and fulfillment of my existence.

Therefore there is only one problem on which all my existence, my peace and my happiness depend: to discover myself in discovering God. If I find Him, I will find myself and if I find my true self I will find Him.

But although this looks simple, it is in reality immensely difficult. In fact if I am left to myself it will be utterly impossible. For although I can know something of God's existence and nature by my own reason, there is no human and rational way in which I can arrive at that contact, that possession of Him, which will be the discovery of Who He really is and of Who I am in Him. . . .

The only One Who can teach me to find God is God, Himself, Alone.

Thomas Merton
(1915-1968)

47

The Lord *is* my shepherd; I shall not want.

He maketh me to lie in green pastures: he leadeth me beside the still waters.

He restoreth my soul: he leadeth me in the paths of righteousness for his name's sake.

Yea, though I walk through the valley of the shadow of death, I will fear no evil: for thou *art* with me; thy rod and thy staff they comfort me.

Thou preparest a table before me in the presence of mine enemies; thou anointest my head with oil; my cup runneth over.

Surely goodness and mercy shall follow me all the days of my life: and I will dwell in the house of the Lord for ever.

> David
> (c.1060 B.C.-c.972 B.C.)
> Psalm 23

Oh, give us pleasure in the flowers today;
And give us not to think so far away
As the uncertain harvest; keep us here
All simply in the springing of the year.

Oh, give us pleasure in the orchard white,
Like nothing else by day, like ghosts by night;
And make us happy in the happy bees,
The swarm dilating round the perfect trees.

And make us happy in the darting bird
That suddenly above the bees is heard,
The meteor that thrusts in with needle bill,
And off a blossom in mid air stands still.

For this is love and nothing else is love,
The which it is reserved for God above
To sanctify to what far ends He will,
But which it only needs that we fulfill.

Robert Frost
(1874-1963)
A Prayer In Spring

Classical sainthood is something more than I hope for (or probably want). At twenty-six I have come to realize that creating a home that is relatively at peace and happy and hopeful is the Christian witness I can best bear. Bringing some comfort and joy into the lives of others is as great a challenge as participating in demonstrations. I can only hope, when my life is finally judged, that I will have done more good than harm, that I will have brought some joy into the lives of my family and friends, that I will have taught my children to respect themselves and other people and to be a part of their times.

Patricia Mohs
(1947-   )

Give us courage, O Lord, to stand up and be counted, to stand up for those who cannot stand up for themselves, to stand up for our- selves when it is needful for us to do so.

Let us fear nothing more than we fear thee.

Let us love nothing more than we love thee, for thus we shall fear nothing also.

Let us have no other God before thee, whether nation or party or state or church. Let us seek no other peace but the peace which is thine, and make us its instruments, opening our eyes and our ears and our hearts, so that we shall know always what work of peace we may do for thee.

Alan Paton
(1903-   )

Be thou blessed and honoured, O my Lady, Virgin Mary, most holy Mother of God, whose most excellent creature thou art. None has ever loved him so tenderly as thou, O glorious Lady. Glory be to thee, my Lady, Virgin Mary, Mother of God, for the same Angel who announced the birth of Christ unto thee also declared thy nativity to thy father and mother, of whose most holy union thou wast conceived and born.

St. Bridget of Sweden
(d.1373)

Hallowed by Thy name,
not mine,
Thy Kingdom come,
not mine,
Thy will be done,
not mine,
Give us peace with Thee
Peace with men
Peace with ourselves,
And free us from all fear.

Dag Hammerskjold
(1905-1961)

There is no great difference in reality between one country and another, because it is always people you meet everywhere. They may look different or be dressed differently, or may have a different education or position; but they are all the same. They are all people to be loved; they are all hungry for love.

Mother Teresa
(1910-   )
A Geography of Compassion

52

O Holy Spirit, come;
Rest on these inarticulate hands and dumb!

Be fire
For my elate desire.

Be wind
To quicken the still music of my mind.

Be the heard
Utter, ineffable word.

Teach, Holy One, with Your love's art
My hands, my heart.

Yours be the tongue
In which the songs of my desire are sung.

> Sister Madeleva
> (1887-1964)
> *Prayer Before Music*

Who has not found the Heaven—below—
Will fail of it above—
For Angels rent the House next ours,
Wherever we remove—

> Emily Dickenson
> (1830-1886)

If I were looking for God, every event and every moment would sow, in my will, grains of His life, that would spring up one day in a tremendous harvest.

For it is God's love that warms me in the sun and God's love that sends the cold rain. It is God's love that feeds me in the bread I eat and God that feeds me also by hunger and fasting. It is the love of God that sends the winter days when I am cold and sick, and the hot summer when I labor and my clothes are full of sweat: but it is God Who breathes on me with light winds off the river and in the breezes out of the wood. His love spreads the shade of the sycamore over my head and sends the water-boy along the edge of the wheatfield with a bucket from the spring, while the laborers are resting and the mules stand under the tree.

It is God's love that speaks to me in the birds and streams but also behind the clamor of the city God speaks to me in His judgments, and all these things are seeds sent to me from His will.

If they would take root in my liberty, and if His will would grow from my freedom, I would become the love that He is, and my harvest would be His glory and my own joy.

And I would grow together with thousands and millions of other freedoms into the gold

and one huge field praising God, loaded with
increase, loaded with corn.

Thomas Merton
(1915-1968)

To Mary Ann Foote

Chicago March 27, 1866

My dear Mrs Foot [*sic*]

The painful announcement, of the severe
illness, of your noble and distinguished husband, has so troubled me, that I cannot
refrain from writing you a few lines, expressive
of my deep sympathy for you, in this your hour
of deep trial, I pray that our Heavenly Father,
may be merciful to you, and restore, the
Senator to health & spare you, the cup of
affliction, which I have been called upon so
freely to receive. I have passed through *such* a
baptism of sorrow, as but few have known,
and my heart, can most readily enter into your
anxious feelings, over the illness, of one so
dear to you and to all the country. In my hours
of deep affliction, I often think it would have
been *some* solace to me and *perhaps* have
lessened the grief, which is now breaking my
heart—if my idolized had passed away, after

an illness, and I had been permitted to watch over him and tend him to the last. No such assuaging thought, comes to my relief and only the knowledge, that no sign of recognition from my dearly beloved husband or a loving parting word or farewell, no such thoughts come to soothe *this* distracted brain.

The prayers, of a suffering woman are yours, that the life of your good husband, may be spared, yet if the Divine will, orders differently, I trust you may be prepared to bow in submission to so terrible a decree. With apologies, for troubling you, with so lengthy a note—when your time and thoughts are so sadly & anxiously occupied. I remain

> truly & affectionately
> Mary Lincoln
> (1818-1882)

O most holy mother of Jesus, thou who didst witness and didst feel the utter desolation of thy divine Son, help me in my hour of need. O mother, I come to bury my anguish in thy heart; and in thy heart to seek courage and strength. O mother, offer me to Jesus.

> St. Bernadette
> (1844-1879)

56

May I have no will of my own, O Lord, but let Thine alone reign in me . . . I ask this of Thee . . . desiring that the strength of Thy love should overpower with its sweet violence all my resistance to its fulfillment.

St. Louise de Marillac
(1591-1660)

Hail, Jesus' Virgin-Mother ever blest,
Alone of women Mother eke and Maid,
Others to thee their several offerings make;
This one brings gold, that silver, while a third
Bears to thy shrine his gift of costly gems.
For these, each craves his boon—one strength
    of limb—
One wealth—one, through his spouse's
    fruitfulness,
The hope a father's pleasing name to bear—
One Nestor's eld would equal. I, poor bard,
Rich in goodwill, but poor in all beside,
Bring thee my verse—nought have I else
    to bring—
And beg, in quital of this worthless gift,
That greatest meed—a heart that feareth God,
And free for aye from sin's foul tyranny.
Erasmus, his vow.

Desiderius Erasmus
(c1466-1536)
Votive Ode
57

We are not expecting utopia here on this earth. But God meant things to be much easier than we have made them. A man has a natural right to food, clothing and shelter. A certain amount of goods is necessary to lead a good life. A family needs work as well as bread. Property is proper to man. We must keep repeating these things. Eternal life begins now. "All the way to heaven is heaven, because He said, 'I am the Way.'" The Cross is there of course, but "in the Cross is joy of spirit." And love makes all things easy. If we are putting off the old man and putting on Christ, then we are walking in love, and love is all what we want. But it is hard to love, from the human standpoint and from the divine standpoint, in a two-room apartment. We are eminently practical, realistic.

Dorothy Day
(1899-   )
All the Way to Heaven

To love life and men as God loves them—
     for the sake of their infinite possibilities,
to wait like Him,
to judge like Him
without passing judgment,
to obey the order when it is given
and never look back—
then He can use you—then, *perhaps,* He will
     use you.

   And if he doesn't use you—what matter. In
His hand, every moment has its meaning, its
greatness, its glory, its peace, its co-inherence.

   From this perspective, to "believe in God"
is to believe in yourself, as self-evident, as
"illogical," and as impossible to explain: if I
can be, then God *is.*

Dag Hammarskjold
(1905-1961)

"Now there stood by the cross of Jesus
          his mother."

O wondrous mother! since the dawn of time
Was ever joy, was ever grief like thine?
Oh! highly favor'd in thy joy's deep flow,
And flavor'd e'en in this, thy bitt'rest woe.

Thou, once, a tender deeply serious maiden,
Through calm, deep loving years, in silence
     grew,

Full of high thought and holy aspiration,
Which, save thy Father, God's, no eye might
    view.

Poor was that home in simple Nazareth
Where thou, fair growing, like some silent
    flower,
Last of a kingly line—unknown and lowly,
A desert lily—pass'd thy childhood's hour.

And then it came—that message from the
    Highest,
Such as to women ne'er before descended;
Th' Almighty's shadowing wings thy soul
    o'erspread,
And with thy life the life of worlds was
    blended.

What visions, then, of future glory fill'd thee.
Mother of King and kingdom yet unknown,
Mother, fulfiller of all prophecy,
Which through dim ages wondr'ing seers
    had shown.

Well did thy dark eye kindle, thy deep soul
Rise into billows, and thy heart rejoice;
Then woke the poet's fire, the prophet's song
Tuned with strange burning words thy timid
    voice.

Then in dark contrast came the lowly manger,
The outcast shed, the tramp of brutal feet;
Again, behold earth's learned and her lowly,
Sages and shepherds prostrate at thy feet.

Then to the temple bearing, hark! again
Those strange conflicting tones of prophecy
Breathe o'er the child, foreshadowing words
        of joy
High triumph, and yet bitter agony.

Oh, highly favor'd thou, in many an hour
Spent in lone musing with thy wondrous son,
When thou didst gaze into that glorious eye,
And hold that mighty hand within thy own.

Bless'd through those thirty years when
        in thy dwelling
He lived a God disguised, with
        unknown power,
And thou, his sole adorer—his best love.
Trusting, revering, waited for his hour.

Bless'd in that hour, when call'd by
        op'ning heaven
With cloud, and voice, and the baptizing
        flame,
Up from the Jordan walk'd the acknowledged
        stranger,
And awe-struck crowds grew silent as he
        came.

Bless'd, when full of grace, with glory crown'd,
He from both hands almighty favors pour'd,
And though he had not where to lay his head,
Brought to his feet alike the slave and lord.

Crowds follow'd; thousands shouted, lo,
        our king!

Fast beat thy heart: now, now the hour
    draws nigh;
Behold the crown—the throne; the nations
    bend:
Ah! no, fond mother, no; behold him die.

Now by that cross thou takest thy final station,
And sharest the last dark trial of thy son;
Not with weak tears . . .
But with high, silent anguish, like his own.

Hail, highly favor'd, even in this deep passion,
Hail, in thy bitter anguish thou art bless'd—
Bless'd in thy holy power with him to suffer,
Those deep death-pangs that lead to higher
    rest.

All now is darkness, and in that deep stillness
The God-man wrestles with that mighty woe:
Hark to that cry, the Rock of Ages rending—
'Tis finish'd! Mother, all is glory now.

By sufferings mighty as his mighty soul
Hath the Jehovah risen—forever bless'd;
And through all ages must his heart-beloved
Through the same baptism enter the same
    roof.

              Harriet Beecher Stowe
              (1811-1896)
              Mary At The Cross

We pray for life and pray for grace;
Let not blindness be with us by day,
Nor impotence our associate by night.
May we be blessed with children,
And may what we plant bear fruit.
Let there be peace in the world,
And may there be prosperity
In this land abundantly.

Okyeame Nana Amoateng

It is not love in the abstract that counts. Men
have loved a cause as they have loved a
woman. Men have loved the brotherhood, the
workers, the poor, the oppressed—but they
have not loved *man,* they have not loved the
least of these. They have not loved "per-
sonally." It is hard to love. It is the hardest
thing in the world, naturally speaking. Have
you ever read Tolstoi's *Resurrection?* He tells
of political prisoners in a long prison train,
enduring chains and persecution for their love
of their brothers, ignoring those same brothers
on the long trek to Siberia. It is never the
brother right next to us, but brothers in the
abstract that are easy to love.

Dorothy Day
(1899-   )
Personal Love

God be in my head,
And in my understanding:
God be in mine eyes,
And in my looking:
God be in my mouth
And in my speaking;
God be in my heart,
And in my thinking;
God be at my end,
And at my departing.

Sixteenth Century Primer

Mary, Mother of God and mother also of those who are trying to draw near to God, pray for me. I want to draw near to God, but feel myself far away from him. When I ask you to pray for me, I mean not only on behalf of me—which is certainly among the favours that I ask—but also *for* me in the sense of in my place. Pray when my prayers fail. Speak to your Son when I am silent; speak to your Son of the things that for one reason or another I am unable to speak about. Ask him for what I need; beg his mercy; give him praise. My dryness will not then leave me destitute but on the contrary leave me richer.

Dom Hubert Van Zeller
(1905-   )

My God, I thank Thee, who hast made
  The earth so bright,
So full of splendour and of joy,
  Beauty and light;
So many glorious things are here,
  Noble and right.

I thank Thee, Lord, that Thou hast kept
  The best in store:
We have enough, yet not too much
  To long for more—
A yearning for a deeper peace
  Not known before.

Adelaide Anne Procter
(1825-1864)

O heavenly Father, subdue in me whatever is
contrary to thy holy will. Grant that I may ever
study to know thy will, that I may know how
to please thee.

Grant, O God, that I may never run into
those temptations which, in my prayers, I
desire to avoid.

Lord never permit my trials to be above my
strength.

Thomas Wilson
(1663-1755)

J oan: Only for my voices I should lose all heart. That is why I had to steal away to pray here alone after the coronation. I'll tell you something, Jack. It is in the bells I hear my voices. Not to-day, when they all rang: that was nothing but jangling. But here in this corner, where the bells come down from heaven, and the echoes linger, or in the fields, where they come from a distance through the quiet of the countryside, my voices are in them. (The cathedral clock chimes the quarter) Hark! (She becomes rapt) Do you hear? "Dear-child-of-God": just what you said. At the half-hour they will say "Be-brave-go-on." At the three-quarters they will say "I-am-thy-Help."

George Bernard Shaw
(1856-1950)
St. Joan

Almighty God, you have given us this good land for our heritage. We humbly ask you that we may always prove ourselves a people mindful of your favor and glad to do your will. Bless our land with honorable endeavor, sound learning and pure manners. Save us from violence, discord and confusion, from pride and arrogance, and from every evil way. Defend our liberties and fashion into one united people the multitude brought here out of many nations and tongues. Endow with the Spirit of wisdom those to whom in your name we entrust the authority of government, that there may be justice and peace at home, and that through obedience to your law we may show forth your praise among the nations on earth. In time of prosperity fill our hearts with thankfulness, and in the day of trouble do not allow our trust in you to fail.   Amen.

Thomas Jefferson
(1743-1826)
Prayer for the Nation

Holy Mary, bring help to the miserable, strengthen those who are afraid, comfort those who mourn, pray for the world at large, plead the cause of the clergy, intercede for devout women. May all who pay homage to your holy name experience your powerful help.

The Breviary
To Our Lady

Make a joyful noise unto the Lord, all ye lands.

Serve the Lord with gladness: come before his presence with singing.

Know ye that the Lord he *is* God: *it is* he *that* hath made us, and not we ourselves; *we are* his people, and the sheep of his pasture.

Enter into his gates with thanksgiving, *and* into his courts with praise: be thankful unto him, *and* bless his name.

For the Lord *is* good; his mercy *is* everlasting; and his truth *endureth* to all generations.

David
(c.1060-972 B.C.)
Psalm 100

I think it must be lonely to be God.
Nobody loves a master. No. Despite
The bright hosannas, bright dear-Lords,
    and bright
Determined reverence of Sunday eyes.

Picture Jehovah striding through the hall
Of His importance, creatures running out
From servant-corners to acclaim, to shout
Appreciation of His merit's glare.

But who walks with Him?—dares to take
    His arm,
To slap Him on the shoulder, tweak His ear,
Buy Him a Coca-Cola or a beer,
Poor-pooh His politics, call Him a fool?

Perhaps—who knows? He tires of looking
    down.
Those eyes are never lifted. Never straight.
Perhaps sometimes He tires of being great
In solitude. Without a hand to hold.

        Gwendolyn Brooks
        (1917-)
        the preacher ruminates
          behind the sermon

Teach us, good Lord, to serve thee as thou
    deservest;
To give and not to count the cost;
To fight and not to heed the wounds;
To toil and not to seek for rest;
To labour and not to ask for any reward
Save that of knowing that we do thy will.

St. Ignatius Loyola
(1491-1556)

O most powerful and glorious Lord God, at
whose command the winds blow, and lift up
the waves of the sea, and who stillest the rage
thereof: We thy creatures, but miserable
sinners, do in this our great distress cry unto
thee for help: Save, Lord, or else we perish.
We confess, when we have been safe, and seen
all things quiet about us, we have forgot thee
our God, and refused to hearken to the still
voice of thy word, and to obey thy command-
ments: But now we see how terrible thou art in
all thy works of wonder; the great God to be
feared above all: And therefore we adore thy
Divine Majesty, acknowledging thy power, and
imploring thy goodness. Help, Lord, and save
us for thy mercy's sake in Jesus Christ thy Son,
our Lord.   Amen.

The Book of Common Prayer

O Lady Mary, thy bright crown
  Is no mere crown of majesty;
For with the reflex of His own
  Resplendent thorns Christ circled thee.

The red rose of this Passion-tide
  Doth take a deeper hue from thee,
In the five wounds of Jesus dyed,
  And in thy bleeding thoughts, Mary!

The soldier struck a triple stroke,
  That smote thy Jesus on the tree:
He broke the Heart of Hearts, and broke
  The Saint's and Mother's heart in thee.

Thy son went up the angels' ways,
  His passion ended; but, ah me!
Thou found'st the road of further days
  A longer way to Calvary:

On the hard cross of hope deferred
  Thou hung'st in loving agony,
Until the mortal-dreaded word
  Which chills *our* mirth, spake mirth to thee.

The angel Death from this cold tomb
  Of life did roll the stone away;
And He thou barest in thy womb
  Caught thee at last into the day,
Before the living throne of Whom
  The Lights of Heaven burning pray.

              Francis Thompson
              (1859-1907)
              The Passion of Mary

O God, it might seem odd to some to pray for someone not yet born—but not to you and not to me.

In these nine months of womanly patience, I have learned more than ever to marvel at your creative plans—and our part in them.

I rejoice that the fashioning of a baby, and the founding of a family, requires the gifts of body, mind and spirit you have given to us each.

Bless these days of waiting, of preparation, of tender hope. Let only things and thoughts that are clean and strong and glad be about us.

I give you thanks that from childhood till this experience of maturity, you have made it both beautiful and natural for me to give love and to receive it.

In this newest experience, hold us each safe, relaxed, and full of eager hope—even as you count each life in your presence, precious. Amen.

Rita Snowden
(1907-   )
Expecting A Baby

Grant, O Lord, that Thy Will may be done in me! That Thy Will may be fulfilled in every way and in every manner that pleases Thee, O my Lord! If Thou dost will it to be in the midst of trials, give me, then, the strength to bear them, and then let come what may. If Thou dost will that there be persecutions, infirmities, humiliations, and want, behold I stand before Thee, O my Father. I will not refuse them. It would not be right to flee from them.

Since Thy Son, speaking in the name of all, has offered Thee my will along with the others, I could not fail on my part to give Thee what He promised in my name. But deign to give me that kingdom of Thine which He requested for me, so that I may be equal to such an undertaking . . .

St. Teresa of Avila
(1515-1582)

O God, help us not to despise or oppose what we do not understand.

William Penn
(1644-1718)

Now is the moment most acceptable
To enter the soul's peace, to rise and go
Into the vast illuminated silence
Of regions that the saints and mystics know.

Let it be said of us: They found God dwelling
Deep in their souls to which they fled
    from pain.
Let it be written on the stones they grant us
When peace shall deign to walk the earth
    again:

These found the hidden places of the tempest
In the soul's fastness, in its long sweet lull,
A generation of the inward vision
Whose outward glance became intolerable.

        Jessica Powers
        (1905-   )
        This Generation of War

And thou that art the flower of virgins all,
Of whom Bernard has such a love to write,
To thee now in beginning first I call!
Comfort of wretched us, help me recite
Thy maiden's death, who, through her merit
    bright,
Won life eternal, vanquishing with glory
The fiend, as men can read here in her story.

Thou daughter of thy son, mother and maid,
Thou well of mercy, sinful souls' physician,
In whom for goodness God to dwell essayed,
Thou humble, yet enthroned in high position,
So didst thou lift our nature with thy mission
That He that made all nature thus was won
To clothe in flesh and blood His only Son.

Within the blissful cloister of thy side
To man's shape grew the eternal Love and
    Peace,
Lord of the three-fold universe, and Guide,
Whom earth and heaven and ocean never cease
To praise, Thou, spotless virgin, for a space,
Bore in thee, maiden still in every feature,
He that Creator was of every creature.

In thee are mercy and magnificence,
Good and pity in such unity
That thou, that art the sun of excellence,
Not only helpest those that pray to thee,
But often times, in thy benignity,

Freely, before men any help petition,
Thou dost appear, and art their lives' physician.

Help me, thou lovely, meek, and blessed maid,
Who banished now in bitterness must dwell;
Think on the wife of Canaan, she who said
That dogs would feed upon the crumbs that fell
Down from their master's table. I know well
that I am sinful, wretched son of Eve,
And yet accept my faith, for I believe.

And since all faith, when lacking works,
        is dead,
So give me now for work both wit and space.
That I from darkness be delivered!
O thou that art so fair and full of grace,
Be advocate for me in that high place
Where there is endless singing of "Hosannah!"
Mother of Christ, dear daughter of St. Anna!

Geoffrey Chaucer
(c. 1340-1400)

*D*oes the darkness cradle thee
Than mine arms more tenderly?
Do the angels God hath put
   There to guard thy lonely sleep—
One at head and one at foot—
   Watch more fond and constant keep?
When the black-bird sings in May,
   And the Spring is in the wood,
Would you never trudge the way
   Over hilltops, if you could?
Was my harp so hard a load
   Even on the sunny morns
When the plumèd huntsmen rode
   To the music of their horns?
Hath the love that lit the stars,
   Fills the sea and moulds the flowers,
Whose completeness nothing mars,
   Made forgot what once was ours?
Christ hath perfect rest to give;
   Stillness and perpetual peace;
You, who found it hard to live,
   Sleep and sleep, without surcease.

Christ hath stars to light thy porch,
   Silence after fevered song;—
I had but a minstrel's torch
   And the way was wet and long.
Sleep. No more on winter nights,
   Harping at some castle gate,

Thou must see the revel lights
   Stream upon our cold estate.
Bitter was the bread of song
   While you tarried in my tent,
And the jeering of the throng
   Hurt you, as it came and went.
When you slept upon my breast
   Grief had wed me long ago:
Christ hath his personal rest
   For thy weariness. But Oh!
When I sleep beside the road,
   Thanking God thou liest not so,
Brother to the owl and toad,
   Could'st thou, Dear, but let me know,
Does the darkness cradle thee
Than mine arms more tenderly?

Willa Cather
(1873-1947)
The Poor Minstrel

Now is my misery full, and namelessly it fills
me. I am stark, as the stone's inside is stark.
Hard as I am, I know but one thing:
You grew—
. . . and grew
in order to stand forth
as too great pain
quite beyond my heart's grasping.
Now you are lying straight across my lap,
now I can no longer
give you birth.

> Rainer Maria Rilke
> (1875-1926)
> *Pietà*

Thanks be to thee, my Lord Jesus Christ,
For all the benefits thou has won for me,
For all the pains and insults thou hast
borne for me.

O most merciful Redeemer, Friend, and
Brother,
May I know thee more clearly,
Love thee more dearly,
And follow thee more nearly:
For ever and ever.   Amen.

> St. Richard of Chichester
> (1197-1253)

I am, says, God, Master of the Three Virtues.

Faith is a faithful wife.
Charity is an ardent mother.
But hope is a tiny girl.

I am, says, God, the Master of Virtues.

Faith is she who remains steadfast during
        centuries and centuries.
Charity is she who gives herself during
        centuries and centuries.
But my little hope is she
Who rises every morning.

I am, says God, the Lord of Virtues.

Faith is she who remains tense during
        centuries and centuries.
Charity is she who unbends during
        centuries and centuries.
But my little hope
is she who every morning
wishes us good day.

*   *   *   *

I am, says God, the Lord of Virtues.

Faith is she who watches during
        centuries and centuries.
Charity is she who watches during
        centuries and centuries.

But my little hope is she
who goes to bed every night
and gets up every morning
and really sleeps very well.

I am, says God, the Lord of that virtue.

My little hope is she
who goes to sleep every night,
in that child's crib of hers,
after having said her prayers properly,
and who every morning wakes up and rises
and says her prayers with a new look
    in her eyes.

I am, says God, Lord of the Three Virtues.

Faith is a great tree, an oak rooted in the
    heart of France.
And under the wings of that tree, Charity,
    my daughter Charity shelters all the
    woes of the world.
And my little hope is nothing but that little
    earnest of a bud which shows itself
    at the beginning of April.

*   *   *   *

Charles Péguy
(1873-1914)
Hope

But, in what concerns our interior life, let nothing be "for the moment only"—let all we do be *everlasting* and *final,* by choosing always what is best, at the actual moment and in the actual circumstances. What strength is given to the soul by such a permanent choice spontaneously made by those who generously embrace the divine will of God! Good God, deliver us from waverers and falterers, for in them the flame of love divine is not yet kindled; and to live in the Sacré-Coeur such is needed!

St. Madeline-Sophie Barat
(1779-1865)

Lord . . . some things I believe, I think. Help my unbelief . . . and all my doubts and misgivings and apprehensions and uncertainties. . . .

Michael McCauley
(1947-   )

Be thou blessed, and praised, and glorified for ever, O my Lord Jesus, who art enthroned in thy heavenly kingdom, in the glory of thy Godhead and with the fulness of that most sacred Humanity which thou didst take from the most pure blood of the Virgin. Even so shalt thou come in the day of judgement to judge the souls of the living and the dead; who livest and reignest with the Father and the Holy Ghost, world without end.

St. Bridget of Sweden
(d.1373)

Savior! I've no one else to tell—
And so I trouble *thee*.
I am the one forgot thee so—
Dost thou remember me?
Nor, for myself, I came so far—
That were the little load—
I brought thee the imperial Heart
I had not strength to hold—
The Heart I carried in my own—
Till mine too heavy grew—
Yet—strangest—*heavier* since it went—
Is it too large for *you?*

Emily Dickinson
(1830-1886)

Father in heaven,
our hearts desire the warmth of your love
and our minds are searching for the light
    of your Word.

Increase our longing for Christ our Savior
and give us the strength to grow in love,
that the dawn of his coming
may find us rejoicing in his presence
and welcoming the light of his truth.

We ask this in the name of Jesus the Lord.
Amen.

        Liturgy, First Sunday of Advent

O Thou Who makest eloquent the tongues of
little ones, instruct my tongue and pour upon
my lips the grace of Thy blessing. Grant me a
keen intellect, a strong memory, method and
facility in learning, subtlety in interpreting
and elegance of speech; enlighten the
beginning, direct the progress, perfect the
issue, Thou Who art true God and true man,
Who livest and reignest forever.   Amen.

        St. Thomas Aquinas
        (1225-1274)
        Prayer Before Study

Lord, what have I that I may offer Thee?
Look, Lord, I pray Thee, and see."—

"What is it thou hast got?
Nay, child, what is it thou hast not?
Thou hast all gifts that I have given to thee:
Offer them all to Me,
The great ones and the small;
I will accept them one and all."—

"I have a will, good Lord, but it is marred;
A heart both crushed and hard:
Not such as these the gift
Clean-handed lovely saints uplift."—

"Nay, child, but wilt thou judge for Me?
I crave not thine, but thee."—

"Ah Lord Who lovest me!
Such as I have now give I thee."

Christina Rossetti
(1830-1894)

Lead, kindly Light, through the encircling
   gloom;
  Lead Thou me on!
The night is dark, and I am far from home;
  Lead Thou me on!
Keep Thou my feet: I do not ask to see
The distant scene; one step enough for me.

I was not ever thus, nor prayed that Thou
   Shouldst lead me on.
I loved to choose and see my path; but now
   Lead Thou me on.
I loved the garish day, and, spite of fears,
Pride ruled my will; remember not past years.

So long Thy power hath blessed me, sure it still
   Will lead me on
O'er moor and fen, o'er crag and torrent, till
   The night is gone,
And in the morn those angel faces smile
Which I have loved long since, and
    lost awhile.

       Cardinal Newman
       (1801-1890)
       The Pillar of the Cloud

Yes, lady, in the bright red suit and careful
grey hair, coming out of nowhere one Sunday
afternoon, coming at me, I have taught my
daughter that God is everywhere
       even when she laughs
       saying, "in my toast,"
       taking a big bite.
God, lady, like sex, is something you can't
avoid so you do what you can. Sometimes she
thinks God is in a big airplane
       digging the clouds
       and an occasional glimpse
       of the ground.
But prayer. That we haven't talked about
because yes, lady, I pray, like Christ himself
prayed, in the garden, that last night, knowing
what lay before, knowing but still hoping there
was a way out, praying for a way out, in sweat
and darkness he prayed. Not the way they
teach you:
       God bless mommy, daddy,
       Bobbie and Jane.
       And please, God, let me
       have a pony for my birthday.
No one teaches you the other, the one you say,
sweating in the dark, the only one you really
need, hopeless and still hoping, on your knees,

pinned there by what you know but still saying
        "let it pass."
No, I will not teach my daughter how to pray.
She will learn it herself. When the time comes.

Kathleen Wiegner
(1938-   )
For the Woman Who Asked
Me If I Believe in God
And If I Pray

May the Lord Jesus touch our eyes,
as he did those of the blind.
Then we shall begin to see
In visible things those which are invisible.
May he open our eyes to gaze,
not on present realities,
but on the blessings to come.
May he open the eyes of our heart
to contemplate God in Spirit,
through Jesus Christ the Lord, to whom
belong power and glory through all eternity.

Adamantius Origen
(c.185-c.254)

I will lift up mine eyes unto the hills, from whence cometh my help.

My help *cometh* from the Lord, which made heaven and earth.

He will not suffer thy foot to be moved: he that keepeth thee will not slumber.

Behold, he that keepeth Is-ra-el shall neither slumber nor sleep.

The Lord *is* thy keeper: the Lord *is* thy shade upon thy right hand.

The sun shall not smite thee by day, nor the moon by night.

The Lord shall preserve thee from all evil: he shall preserve thy soul.

The Lord shall preserve thy going out and thy coming in from this time forth, and even for evermore.

David
(c.1060 B.C.-972 B.C.)
Psalm 121

In the place of abtruse theological specu-
lations and noisy indulgences in chapel
practices in general, my father possessed a
consuming and invincible love of God, Who,
he believed, knew "no variableness neither
shadow of turning" and Who had formed us
all to fear Him, to worship Him, and, in so far
as each was able, to work out His purposes for
all men upon the earth. He was not interested
in trying to prove God's existence, which, he
said, was impossible and, therefore, a foolish
waste of time, or in defining Him, which had
been attempted not very successfully through
the centuries only by human beings like
ourselves. He simply staked all that he had,
and was, on a tremendous gamble that God
lived and moved among us and that His active
concern for His world and for all His creatures
was constant, invulnerable, and unfailing.
When the exciting question had arisen as to a
name for my brother Ansie, my father insisted
on calling him Anselm after a saint, who, he
claimed, had done more for his peace of mind
and ways of thought and action than had any
other philosopher or teacher throughout all
recorded time. This St. Anselm had contended
and taught that a simple belief in God would
in the end bring some understanding of Him;

indeed, that no understanding whatever was possible without an initial and perhaps even reckless casting aside of all one's unanswerable questions, doubts, and fears.

Mary Ellen Chase
(1887-1973)
The Lovely Ambition

I pray to you, my God,
and call you by your name,
but cannot lay hold of you
because you are greater than a name
and smaller than a word,
more silent than all silence in the world.
Make me receptive to you,
give me a living heart
and new eyes
to see you, hidden and invisible,
to take you as you are
when you come without power,
and, in my weakness, in my death,
to know who you are.

Huub Oosterhuis
(1933-   )

In the hour of my distress,
When temptations me oppress,
And when I my sins confess,
    Sweet Spirit comfort me!

When I lie within my bed,
Sick in heart and sick in head,
And with doubts discomforted,
    Sweet Spirit comfort me!

When the house doth sigh and weep,
And the world is drowned in sleep,
Yet mine eyes the watch do keep,
    Sweet Spirit comfort me!

When the artless Doctor sees
Not one hope but of his fees,
And his skill runs on the lees,
    Sweet Spirit comfort me!

When his potion and his pill,
His, or none, or little skill,
Meet for nothing but to kill,
    Sweet Spirit comfort me!

When the passing-bell doth toll,
And the Furies in a shoal,
Come to fright a parting soul,
    Sweet Spirit comfort me!

When the tapers now burn blue,
And the comforters are few,

And that number more than true,
   Sweet Spirit comfort me!

When the priest his last hath prayed,
And I nod to what is said,
'Cause my speech is now decayed,
   Sweet Spirit comfort me!

When (God knows) I'm tossed about,
Either with despair or doubt,
Yet before the glass be out,
   Sweet Spirit comfort me!

When the Tempter me pursu'th
With the sins of all my youth,
And half damns me with untruth,
   Sweet Spirit comfort me!

When the flames and hellish cries
Fright mine ears and fright mine eyes,
And all terrors me surprise,
   Sweet Spirit comfort me!

When the judgment is revealed,
And that opened which was sealed,
When to thee I have appealed,
   Sweet Spirit comfort me!

Robert Herrick
(1591-1674)
*His Litany to the
Holy Spirit*

O God, who didst lead Abraham out of Ur of the Chaldees, and didst preserve thy servant from harm . . . deign we beseech thee to watch over us thy servants. Be unto us, O Lord . . . a comfort on the way, a shade in the heat, a shelter in the rain and cold, a sure transport in our weariness, a refuge in trouble, a staff upon uncertain ground, a harbour in shipwreck; so that with thee as our leader we may arrive happily at our destination and at length return safely to our homes.

The Breviary

O Lord, calm the waves of this heart; calm its tempests! Calm thyself, O my soul, so that the divine can act in thee! Calm thyself, O my soul, so that God is able to repose in thee, so that His peace may cover thee! Yes, Father in Heaven, often have we found that the world cannot give us peace, O but make us feel that Thou art able to give peace; let us know the truth of Thy promise: that the whole world may not be able to take away Thy peace.

Sören Kierkegaard
(1813-1855)
For Thy Peace

Lord, thou knowest better than I that I am growing older and will some day be old. Keep me from the fatal habit of thinking that I must say something on every subject and on every occasion.

Release me from craving to straighten out everybody's affairs. Make me thoughtful but not moody; helpful but not bossy.

With my vast store of wisdom it seems a pity not to use it all, but thou knowest, Lord, that I want a few friends at the end.

Keep my mind free from the recital of endless detail; give me wings to get to the point. Seal my lips on my aches and pains. They are increasing, and love of rehearsing them is becoming sweeter as the years go by. I dare not ask for grace enough to enjoy the tales of other's pains, but help me to endure them with patience.

I dare not ask for improved memory but for a growing humility, and a lessening of cock-sureness when my memory seems to clash with the memories of others. Teach me the glorious lesson that occasionally I may be mistaken.

Keep me reasonably sweet; I do not want to be a saint—some of them are so hard to live with—but a sour old person is one of the crowning works of the devil.

Give me the ability to see good things in unexpected places and talents in unexpected people; and give me, Lord, the grace to tell them so.   Amen.

17th Century Nun's Prayer

It was a glimpse of truths divine
  Unto my spirit given,
Illumined by a ray of light
  That shone direct from Heaven!

I felt there was a God on high
  By whom all things were made;
I saw His wisdom and His power
  In all His works displayed.

But most throughout the moral world
  I saw His glory shine;
I saw His wisdom infinite,
  His mercy all divine.

Anne Brontë
(1820-1849)
In Memory of a
Happy Day in
February

That I might bless the Lord
Who conserves all—
Heaven with its countless bright orders,
Land, strand and flood,
That I might search the books all
That would be good for any soul;
At times kneeling to beloved Heaven
At times psalm-singing;
At times contemplating the King of Heaven,
Holy the Chief;
At times at work without compulsion,
This would be delightful;
At times picking kelp from the rocks
At times fishing
At times giving food to the poor
At times in a carcair (solitary cell).

St. Columba
(c.521-597)

O Heart of love, I put all my trust in thee.
For I fear all things from my own weakness,
but I hope for all things from thy goodness.

St. Margaret Mary
(1647-1690)

O Lord, in me there lieth nought
 But to thy search revealed lies;
  For when I sit
  Thou markest it;
 No less thou notest when I rise;
Yea, closest closet of my thought
 Hath open windows to thine eyes.

Thou walkest with me when I walk;
 When to my bed for rest I go,
  I find thee there
  And everywhere;
 Not youngest thought in me doth grow,
No, not one word I cast to talk,
 But, yet unuttered, thou dost know.

If forth I march, thou goest before;
 If back I turn, thou comest behind;
  So forth nor back
  Thy guard I lack;
 Nay, on me too thy hand I find.
Well I thy wisdom may adore,
 But never reach with earthy mind.

To shun thy notice, leave thine eye,
 O! whither might I take my way?

To starry sphere?
Thy throne is there.
To dead men's undelightsome stay?
There is thy walk, and there to lie
Unknown in vain I should assay.

O sun, whom light nor flight can match,
Suppose thy lightful flightful wings
Thou lend to me,
And I could flee
So far as thee the evening brings,
Even led to west he would me catch,
Nor should I lurk with western things.

Do thou thy best, O secret night,
In sable veil to cover me,
Thy sable veil
Shall vainly fail;
With day unmasked my night shall be;
For night is day, and darkness light,
O Father of all lights, to thee.

Mary Herbert,
Countess of Pembroke
(1561-1611)
Psalm 139

Come down, O Christ, and help me! reach
      thy hand,
   For I am drowning in a stormier sea
   Than Simon on thy lake of Galilee:
The wine of life is spilt upon the sand,
My heart is as some famine-murdered land
   Whence all good things have perished
      utterly,
   And well I know my soul in Hell must lie
If I this night before God's throne should
      stand.
"He sleeps perchance, or rideth to the chase,
   Like Baal, when his prophets howled that
      name
   From morn till noon on Carmel's smitten
      height."
Nay, peace, I shall behold before the night,
   The feet of brass, the robe more white
      than flame,
   The wounded hands, the weary human face.

Oscar Wilde
(1854-1900)
E Tenebris

No coward soul is mine
No trembler in the world's storm-troubled
    sphere
I see Heaven's glories shine
And Faith shines equal arming me from Fear

O God within my breast
Almighty ever-present Deity
Life, that in me hast rest
As I Undying Life, have power in Thee

Vain are the thousand creeds
That move men's hearts, unutterably vain,
Worthless as withered weeds
Or idlest froth amid the boundless main

To waken doubt in one
Holding so fast by thy infinity
So surely anchored on
The steadfast rock of Immortality

With wide-embracing love
Thy spirit animates eternal years
Pervades and broods above,
Changes, sustains, dissolves, creates
    and rears

Though Earth and moon were gone
And suns and universes ceased to be
And thou wert left alone

Every Existence would exist in thee

There is not room for Death
Nor atom that his might could render void
Since thou art Being and Breath
And what thou art may never be destroyed.

Emily Brontë
(1818-1848)

*The above, according to Charlotte Brontë,
contains the last lines that her sister, Emily,
wrote.*

A Wife's Prayer

Lord, I thank you for the husband you have
given me. Thank you for the joys of loving
him, for the warmth that comes from his love,
and for our children, the fruit of that love.
Help me to appreciate the beauty of our
sacrament and the tender moments that have
passed between us. Help me to remember
always that he has given me what he has given
no other—himself, his love, and his children. I
beg the grace to make his life as happy as he
has made mine. Let our love bring us together
to your heart, and with our children around
us, let us adore you forever.   Amen.

I declare before you all that my whole life, whether it be long or short, shall be devoted to your service and the service of the great Imperial Family to which we all belong. But I shall not have strength to carry out this resolution alone unless you join in it with me, as I now invite you to do. God help me to make good my vow, and God bless all of you who are willing to share in it.

Queen Elizabeth II
(1926-   )

I didn't go to church today.
I trust the Lord to understand
The surf was swirling blue and white,
The children swirling on the sand.
He knows, He knows how brief my stay,
How brief this spell of summer weather,
He knows when I am said and done
We'll have a plenty of time together.

Ogden Nash
(1902-1971)
*I Didn't Go
To Church Today*

Lord behold our family here assembled.
We thank Thee for this place in which
    we dwell,
for the love that unites us,
for the peace accorded us this day,
for the hope with which we expect the morrow,
for the health, the work, the food
and the bright skies that make our
    lives delightful,
for our friends in all parts of the earth.

Robert Louis Stevenson
(1850-1894)

Let us pray
for all people of all ages,
for all who, young and old,
belong to each other
and go through life together.
Let us pray
that we may care for
and respect each other,
that we may not be divided,
but may with one mind try
to achieve happiness.

Let us pray
for all children,
for all among us who
are defenseless and small—
for a happy childhood.
Let us pray
that nothing may harm them,
that their lives may not become
distorted and perverse,
that we do not give them scandal
or teach them to hate,
but that we may lead them
to know the truth,
that we may have the courage
to protect the vulnerable,
the immature, the inexperienced
among us.

Let us pray
for our young people

whose lives lie ahead of them
that they may go forward
with open and receptive minds
to meet their future,
that they may learn to live
with life's uncertainties
and face up to disappointments,
that they may learn to accept themselves
and not lose heart.

We pray for all young people,
that they may be generous and honest
toward their parents,
that they do not write off or hate
the older generation,
but respect the past,
and, above all, that they should be
faithful to their friends
and unselfish in love,
that they may not indulge
in what is cheap and futile,
that they may not ruin the lives of others,
but be ready to make this world
a better place to live in.
We ask these things for them
of the Lord our God.

Huub Oosterhuis
(1933-   )

Why all of this, my Lord and my God? Either bring the world to an end or remedy these evils! No heart can support this any longer. I beseech Thee, O Eternal Father, do not permit any more of this. Stop this ravaging fire, O Lord, Thou canst do so, if Thou dost wish. Remember, Lord, Thy Son! Out of respect for Him, then, put an end to all of these ignominies, abominations, and insults. His beauty and His purity do not merit to be thus outraged.

O Lord, we do request this solely for the love of Thy own Son and for ourselves, since we are not entitled to it. We could never dare to petition that He no longer remain in our midst, for what would happen to us then? If there is anything that can make reparation to Thy outraged Majesty, it is precisely this Divine Pledge of Thy mercy, Whom we possess as our own. But, O my God, there must be a remedy for this evil. Deign Thou to apply it!

> St. Teresa of Avila
> (1515-1582)
> *Outrages to the Divine Majesty*

When the heart is hard and parched up,
    come upon me with a shower of mercy.
When grace is lost from life, come with a
    burst of song.
When tumultuous work raises its din on all
    sides, shutting me out from beyond,
    come to me, my Lord of silence,
    with thy peace and rest.
When my beggarly heart sits crouched,
    shut up in a corner, break open the door,
    my king, and come with the ceremony
    of a king.
When desire blinds the mind with delusion
    and dust, O thou holy One, thou wakeful,
come with thy light and with thy thunder.

Rabindranath Tagore
(1861-1941)

May He banish from the hearts of men whatever might endanger peace, may He transform them into witnesses of truth, justice and brotherly love! May He enlighten the rulers of peoples so that in addition to their solicitude for the proper welfare of their citizens, they may guarantee and defend the great gift of peace; may He enkindle the wills of all, so that they may overcome the barriers that divide, cherish the bonds of mutual charity, understand others, and pardon those who have done them wrong; by virtue of His action, may all peoples of the earth become as brothers, and may the most longed-for peace blossom forth and reign always between them!

John XXIII
(1881-1963)
Pacem in Terris

Ere God made us, He loved us; which love was never slacked, nor never shall. And in this love He hath done all His works: and in this love He hath made all things profitable to us: and in this love our life is everlasting: in our making we had beginning: but the love wherein He made us was in Him from without beginning. In which love we have our beginning. And all this shall we see in God without end.

Dame Julian of Norwich
(1343-1443)

Teach me, O God, not to torture myself, not to make a martyr out of myself through stifling reflection, but rather teach me to breathe deeply in faith.

Sören Kierkegaard
(1813-1855)
For Faith

Here in a world of doubt,
A sorrowful abode,
O how my heart and flesh cry out
For Thee, the living God.

Dorothea Dix
(1802-1887)
Meditations for Private Hours

Dear God,
Be good to me,
The sea is so wide
And my boat is so small.

Breton Fishermen's Prayer

God, who hast made all creatures for thy own glory, and has continued all the things of this world for the service of mankind, bless, we pray thee, this machine built for our travel, that it may serve—without loss or danger—for spreading ever more widely the praise and glory of thy name, and for the quicker despatch of the world's affairs; and may foster in the hearts of those who travel in it a yearning for the things above, through Christ our Lord.

Prayer in Aer Lingus Planes

But if you have a huge family, a succession of extra (problem) children, and a necessarily big home with no money for domestic help, and if on top of that write and lecture to help pay for it all (my husband being a school master) when and how—if at all—do you pray? And, in a sense, why? Surely doing all that is *enough?* God can't ask the impossible.

The short answer is that it's impossible if you *don't* pray, as I discovered, because for a long time I didn't.

> Patricia Mohs
> (1947-   )

Make us to remember, O God, that every day is thy gift, and ought to be used according to thy command; through Jesus Christ our Lord.

> Samuel Johnson
> (1709-1784)

O God, I acknowledge Thee to be my creator, my governor, and the source of all good things. I thank Thee for all Thy blessings, but especially for letting me live in the happiest possible society, and practice what I hope is the truest religion. If I am wrong, and if some other religion or social system would be better and more acceptable to Thee, I pray Thee in Thy goodness to let me know it, for I am ready to follow wherever Thou shalt lead me. But if our system is indeed the best, and my religion the truest, then keep me faithful to both of them, and bring the rest of humanity to adopt the same way of life, and the same religious faith—unless the present variety of creeds is part of Thy inscrutable purpose. Grant me an easy death, when Thou takest me to Thyself. I do not presume to suggest whether it should be late or soon. But if it is Thy will, I would much rather come to Thee by a most painful death, than be kept too long away from Thee by the most pleasant of earthly lives.

St. Thomas More
(1478-1535)
Utopia

Let all thy creatures serve thee: because thou
hast spoken, and they were made: thou didst
send forth thy spirit, and they were created,
and there is no one that can resist thy voice.

Book of Judith

Give me whatever you ask of me,
then ask of me what you will, Lord.
Remember that we are only dust,
for of the dust you made us!
But I can do anything in him
who strengthens me;
Lord, strengthen me, and I can do everything!
Give me whatever you ask of me,
then ask of me what you will.

St. Augustine
(354-430)

No matter,—whether known or unknown—-
misjudged, or the contrary,—I am resolved
not to write otherwise. I shall bend as my
powers tend. The two human beings who
understood me, and whom I understood, are
gone: I have some that love me yet, and whom
I love, without expecting, or having a right to
expect, that they shall perfectly understand
me. I am satisfied; but I must have my own
way in the matter of writing. The loss of what
we possess nearest and dearest to us in this
world, produces an effect upon the character:
we search out what we have yet left that can
support, and, when found, we cling to it with
a hold of new-strung tenacity. The faculty of
imagination lifted me when I was sinking,
three months ago; its active exercise has kept
my head above water since; its results cheer me
now, for I feel they have enabled me to give
pleasure to others. I am thankful to God, who
gave me the faculty; and it is for me a part of
my religion to defend this gift, and to profit by
its possession.—Yours sincerely,

Charlotte Brontë
(1816-1855)
Letter to W. S. Williams, Esq.
(Publisher)

One young life lost, two happy young lives blighted,
    With earthward eyes we see:
With eyes uplifted, keener, farther-sighted,
    We look, Oh Lord, to Thee.

Grief hears a funeral knell: Hope hears the ringing
    Of birthday bells on high;
Faith, Hope, and Love, make answer with soft singing,
    Half carol and half cry.

Stoop to console us, Christ, sole consolation,
    While dust returns to dust;
Until that blessed day when all Thy nation
    Shall rise up of the Just.

Christina Rossetti
(1830-1894)
A Death of a First-Born

Can I see another's woe,
And not be in sorrow too.
Can I see another's grief,
And not seek for kind relief.

* * * *

And can he who smiles on all
Hear the wren with sorrows small,
Hear the small bird's grief and care
Hear the woes that infants bear—

And not sit beside the nest
Pouring pity in their breast.
And not sit the cradle near
Weeping tear on infant's tear.

And not sit both night and day,
Wiping all our tears away.
O! no never can it be.
Never never can it be.

He doth give his joy to all.
He becomes an infant small.
He becomes a man of woe
He doth feel the sorrow too.

Think not, thou canst sigh a sigh,
And thy maker is not by.
Think not, thou canst weep a tear,
And thy maker is not near.

O! he gives to us his joy,

That our grief he may destroy
Till our grief is fled and gone
He doth sit by us and moan.

William Blake
(1757-1827)
On Another's Sorrow

Lord Jesus,
you know our regular routine,
the way we pant and puff
to get everything done,
the crushing weight of days
that are too filled—
or perhaps too empty.

This is vacation time . . .
May our joy
find full measure in you!

Pierre Talec

May our home be consecrated, Oh God, by
the light of Thy countenance. May it shine
upon us all in blessing, that these lights may
be to us as the light of love and truth, the light
of peace and good will.   Amen.

Kiddush

Soul of Jesus sanctify me
Blood of Jesus wash me
Passion of Jesus comfort me
Wounds of Jesus hide me
Heart of Jesus receive me
Spirit of Jesus enliven me
Goodness of Jesus pardon me
Beauty of Jesus draw me
Humility of Jesus humble me
Peace of Jesus pacify me
Love of Jesus inflame me
Kingdom of Jesus come to me
Grace of Jesus replenish me
Mercy of Jesus pity me
Sanctity of Jesus sanctify me
Purity of Jesus purify me
Cross of Jesus support me
Nails of Jesus hold me
Mouth of Jesus bless me in life,
    in death, in time and eternity
in the hour of death defend me
—call me to come to thee,
receive me with thy saints in
    glory evermore.
Unite me to thyself O adorable
Victim—life giving heavenly bread
feed me; sanctify me—reign in me,
transform me to thyself; live in me, let
me live in thee, let me adore thee in
thy life giving Sacrament as my God—

listen to thee as to my Master—obey
thee as my King—imitate thee as my
model—follow thee as my shepherd—
love thee as my Father—see thee as
my physician who will heal all the
maladies of my soul—be indeed my
Way, Truth and Life—sustain me O
Heavenly Manna through the desert of
this world, till I shall behold thee
unveiled in thy Glory.

> St. Elizabeth Seton
> (1774-1821)
> Paraphrase of *The Loving Prayer
> of St. Ignatius Loyola*

Lord,
our help and guide,
make your love the foundation of our lives.
May our love for you express itself
in our eagerness to do good for others.

Grant this through our Lord Jesus
      Christ, your Son,
who lives and reigns with you and the
      Holy Spirit,
one God, for ever and ever.

> Liturgy, 28th Sunday

Father in heaven,
the hand of your loving kindness
powerfully yet gently guides all the moments
    of our day.
Go before us in our pilgrimage of life,
anticipate our needs and prevent our falling.

Liturgy, 28th Sunday

We may not look at our pleasure to go to
heaven in feather-beds; it is not the way, for
our Lord himself went thither with great pain
and by many tribulations, which was the path
wherein he walked thither, for the servant may
not look to be in better case than his master.

St. Thomas More
(1478-1535)

If I am not [in God's grace], may God put me
there; and if I am, may God so keep me. I
should be the saddest creature in the world if I
knew I were not in his grace.

St. Joan of Arc
(1412-1431)
Trial Proceedings

How can our minds and bodies be
Grateful enough that we have spent
Here in this generous room, we three,
This evening of content?
Each one of us has walked through storm
And fled the wolves along the road;
But here the hearth is wide and warm,
And for this shelter and this light
Accept, O Lord, our thanks to-night.

Sara Teasdale
(1884-1933)
Grace Before Sleep

O Thou, from whom to be turned is to fall,
    to whom to be turned is to rise,
    and in whom to stand is to abide for ever;
Grant us
    in all our duties thy help;
    in all our perplexities thy guidance;
    in all our dangers thy protection;
    and in all our sorrows thy peace:
        through Jesus Christ our Lord.   Amen.

St. Augustine
(354-430)

Lord, many are tired and lonely;

Teach us to be their friends.

Many are anxious and afraid;

Help us to calm their fears.

Some are tortured in body and mind;

Imbue them with courage and strength

Others in their emptiness seek only wealth, fame, or power;

Teach them to value other gifts than these.

Some are drained of faith: they are cynical, bored, or despairing;

Let our faith shine forth for them to see, that through us they may come to know Your love.

And some live with death in their souls: they are stunned, violent, and filled with hate.

Give us wisdom to save them from the wastelands of the spirit.

And teach us to show our love; let compassion and knowledge combine for the welfare of all Your children—

They all may know they are not alone.

*Gates of Prayer
The New Union Prayerbook*

A ve Maria! maiden mild!
  Listen to a maiden's prayer!
Thou canst hear though from the wild,
  Thou canst save amid despair.
Safe may we sleep beneath thy care,
  Though banished, outcast, and reviled—
Maiden! hear a maiden's prayer;
  Mother, hear a suppliant child!
        Ave Maria!

        Sir Walter Scott
        (1771-1832)
        Hymn to the Virgin

Lord, when my heart was whole
    I kept it back
    And grudged to give it Thee.
Now then that it is broken,
    must I lack
    Thy kind word "Give it me"?
Silence would be but just, and
    Thou art just.
Yet since I lie here shattered in the dust,
    With still an eye to lift to Thee,
A broken heart to give,
I think that Thou wilt bid me live,
    And answer "Give it Me."

Christina Rossetti
(1830-1894)

Give us courage and gaiety and the quiet mind. Spare us to our friends, soften us to our enemies. Bless us, if it may be, in all our innocent endeavours. If it may not, give us strength to encounter that which is to come, that we may be brave in peril, constant in tribulation, temperate in wrath, and in all changes of fortune, and, down even to the gates of death, loyal and loving to one another: through Jesus Christ our Lord.   Amen.

> Robert Louis Stevenson
> (1850-1894)

God permits industrious Angels—
Afternoons—to play—
I met one—forgot my Schoolmates—
All—for Him—straightway—
God calls home—the Angels—promptly—
At the Setting Sun—
I missed mine—how *dreary—Marbles—*
After playing Crown!

> Emily Dickinson
> (1830-1886)

Saint Nicholas

Might I, if you can find it, be given
a chameleon with tail
that curls like a watch spring; and vertical
on the body—including the face—pale
tiger-stripes, about seven;
(the melanin in the skin
having been shaded from the sun by thin
bars; the spinal dome
beaded along the ridge
as if it were platinum)?

If you can find no striped chameleon,
might I have a dress or suit
I guess you have heard of it of giviut?
and to wear with it, a taslon shirt, the drip-
dry fruit of research second to none;
sewn, I hope, by Excello;
as for buttons to keep down the collar-
points, no.
The shirt could be white—
and be "worn before six,"
either in daylight or at night.

But don't give me, if I can't have the dress,
a trip to Greenland, or grim
trip to the moon. The moon should come here.
Let him make the trip down, spread on
my dark floor some dim marvel, and if a
success

that I stoop to pick up and wear,
I could ask nothing more. A thing yet
   more rare,
      though, and different,
         would be this: Hans von Marees'
      St. Hubert, kneeling with head bent,
   erect—in velvet and tense with restraint—
hand hanging down: the horse, free.
Not the original, of course. Give me
a postcard of the scene—huntsman and
      divinity—
   hunt-mad Hubert startled into a saint
      by a stag with a Figure entwined.
      But why tell you what you must have
         divined?
         Saint Nicholas, O Santa Claus,
            would it not be the most
         prized gift that ever was!

         Marianne Moore
         (1887-1972)

The days are growing noticeably shorter; the nights are longer, deeper, colder. Today the sun did not rise as high in the sky as it did yesterday. Tomorrow it will be still lower. At the winter solstice the sun will go below the horizon, below the dark. The sun does die. And then, to our amazement, the Son will rise again.

Come, Lord Jesus, quickly come
In your fearful innocence.
We fumble in the far-spent night
Far from lovers, friends, and home:
Come in your naked, newborn might.
Come, Lord Jesus, quickly come;
My heart withers in your absence.

Come, Lord Jesus, small, enfleshed
Like any human, helpless child.
Come once, come once again, come soon:
The stars in heaven fall, unmeshed;
The sun is dark, blood's on the moon.
Come, word who came to us enfleshed,
Come speak in joy untamed and wild.

Come, thou wholly other, come,
Spoken before words began,
Come and judge your uttered world
Where you made our flesh your home.
Come, with bolts of lightning hurled,
Come, thou wholly other, come,
Who came to man by being man.

Come, Lord Jesus, at the end,
Time's end, my end, forever's start.
Come in your flaming, burning power.
Time, like the temple veil, now rend;
Come, shatter every human hour.
Come, Lord Jesus, at the end.
Break, then mend the waiting heart.

We have much to be judged on when he comes, slums and battlefields and insane asylums, but these are the symptoms of our illness, and the result of our failures in love. In the evening of life we shall be judged on love, and not one of us is going to come off very well, and were it not for my absolute faith in the loving forgiveness of my Lord I could not call on him to come.

Madeleine L'Engle
(1918-   )

I adhere totally to the mysteries of the Christian faith, with the only kind of adherence that seems to me appropriate for mysteries. This adherence is love, not affirmation. Certainly I belong to Christ—or so I hope and believe.

Simone Weil
(1909-1943)

Dear Heart of the Eternal Rose—
  O Many-coloured Heart of Fire—
That in our Lord's green garden grows,
  Come, Holy Ghost, our souls inspire.

Sweet Honey of the heavenly flowers,
  Distilled from the white lily's heart,
Drip on these thirsty lips of ours—
  Thou the anointing Spirit art.

O Wind, down heaven's long lanes ablow,
  Warm, perfume-laden Breath of Love,
O Sweetness, on our hearts bestow
  Thy blessed unction from above.

A Sun, in the mild skies ashine,
  O Moon, bewitching all the night,
These dark and groping ways of mine
  Enable with perpetual light.

Dear Absolution of the Sun,
  Dear Quickener of the meadow's grace,
When the day's course of toil is run,
  Anoint and cheer our soiled face.

When evening falls and darkness creeps,
  And the long starry hours have come,
And all the world is tired, and sleeps,
  Keep far our foes, give peace at home.

O Sun, O Wind, O Flower, O Fire! . . .
Come, Holy Ghost, our souls inspire!

            Sheila Kaye-Smith
            (1887-1956)
            Pentecost